BEST EVER Student COOKBOOK

By Sally Hartland

BROWN DOG BOOKS

Over 50 fast, fabulous, foolproof recipes and ideas that will provide tasty meals for student life and beyond with space for your own all-time favourites. Use the free pages to add much loved recipes and favourite photos to create your own amazing personal cookery journal. Enjoy the journey but remember...

'Never eat more than you can lift' - Miss Piggy

For all students everywhere,

'At the end of the day, the path curves back towards the trough' – Mason Cooley

ISBN 978 190305 634 9

Copyright © 2010 Sally Hartland

First published in the UK in 2010 by
Brown Dog Books
Bath BA1 1JB

Reprinted 2012, 2013, 2016

Designed and illustrated by Grace J. Ward

Food Editor Sue Ashworth

Produced in the UK
Printed in China

Contents

Proper Main Meals:

The Full-on Fry-up
Easy Chicken Curry
Perfect Prawn Curry
Simple Thai Green Curry
'Laugh Often, Dream Big & Reach for the Stars' Space for your favourite photos/recipes
Chilli Con Carne
Chicken & Rice in a Pot
Chipolatas with Cherry Toms
Lemon & Chicken Risotto
'Chaos, panic, pandemonium – my work here is done' Space for your favourite photos/recipes
Pasta with Peas & Ham
Pasta with Tasty Tomato Sauce
Bolognese
Vegetarian Bolognese
'Always be sincere, even if you don't mean it' Space for your favourite photos/recipes
Pasta Bake
Pan Haggerty
Simple Sausage & Potato Casserole
Vegetable Casserole
'Everybody makes mistakes...' Space for your favourite photos/recipes
Wheeler's Beef Stew & Dumplings
Sticky Onion Marmalade Sausages
Mash
Pan-Fried Gammon
'Food for thought is no substitute for the real thing' Space for your favourite photos/recipes
Roast Chicken
Roast Potatoes
Chicken soup
Potato & Roots Hash
'I'm sick of following my dreams...' Space for your favourite photos/recipes

Cauliflower Cheese
Stuffed Peppers
'Heard there was a party. Came.' Space for your favourite photos/recipes

Biscuits, Puddings & Cakes:

Pancakes!
Fab Fruity Flapjacks
No-Bake Fridge Cake
Fat Rascals
'Life is uncertain… eat dessert first.' Space for your favourite photos/recipes
Jumbles
Bread & Butter Pudding
Baked Bananas
Coffee & Walnut Cake
'Map out your future, but do it in pencil.' Space for your favourite photos/recipes
Carrot Cake
Raspberry Muffins
'Just about a month from now…' Space for your favourite photos/recipes

Store Cupboard Items

It is definitely a good idea to get these store cupboard essentials (and the tools) at the beginning of your student year. These can be expensive when living on a student loan, so make a list with your housemates of who buys what. Next, try and persuade a parent to help with these basics - after all, they do have unconditional love!

Good Old Basics

Couscous
Eggs
Flour/cornflour
Noodles
Olive oil/Vegetable oil
Pasta
Rice
Sugar

Essential Cans

Beans such as baked, kidney, black eyed, borlotti, (great for casseroles)
Chopped tomatoes
Corned beef
Lentils
Tuna

Must-have Sauces

Brown sauce
Mango chutney
Onion marmalade
Soy sauce
Teriyaki sauce for stir-fries
Tomato sauce
Worcestershire sauce

Spices & Flavourings

Curry powder
Cinnamon (ground)
Chilli powder
Fresh root ginger (great for stir-fries)
Garlic bulbs
Mustard
Nutmeg (ground)
Oregano (dried)
Salt & black pepper
Stock cubes
Tomato purée
Turmeric (ground)

Other Useful Stuff

Desiccated coconut
Foil
Food wrap
Greaseproof paper
Naan bread/pitta bread
Parmesan cheese (vital for pasta)
Raisins
Walnuts (for Waldorf Salad and Coffee &
Walnut Cake)

Tools for the Job

Baking sheet
Casserole dish
Chopping board
Cook's measuring spoons
Fish slice (but not just for fish)
Frying pan (non-stick)
Garlic crusher
Grater
Kitchen scissors
Knives (Bread knife, cook's knife and small knife)
Measuring jug
Muffin tin
Potato peeler
Roasting tin
Saucepans with lids
Scales
Slotted spoon
Square cake tin

Stick blender (for soups and smoothies)
Toaster
Whisk (electric hand whisk is really useful, or
use a balloon whisk)
Wok
Wooden spoon

Oven Temperatures

Cool

140°C = fan oven 120°C = Gas Mark 1
150°C = fan oven 130°C = Gas Mark 2

Moderate

170°C = fan oven 150°C = Gas Mark 3
180°C = fan oven 160°C = Gas Mark 4
190°C = fan oven 170°C = Gas Mark 5

Hot

200°C = fan oven 180°C = Gas Mark 6
220°C = fan oven 200°C = Gas Mark 7

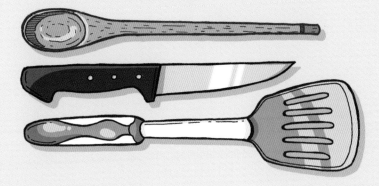

Quick Bites & Tasty Snacks

Welsh Rarebit
Spanish Omelette
Good Old Scrambled Eggs
Piperade
Lush Mushrooms on Toast
The Ever Faithful Bacon Butty
Fish Finger Sarnies
Great Big Chunky Oven Chips
Hot Dogs with Tomato & Pepper Relish
Pitta Bread Pizzas
Garlic Bread
Bubble & Squeak
Jacket Potatoes
Quick Chicken Noodles
Speedy Tuna Pasta
Corned Beef Hash
Wonderful Waldorf Salad
Warm Potato, Green Bean & Cherry Tomato Salad

Welsh Rarebit
Serves 1

This is a classic Welsh recipe that provides a flavoursome snack that will hit the spot when you need something quick.

Preheat the grill to medium.

Put the grated cheese and beer into a small saucepan and melt slowly over a medium heat, stirring continuously with a wooden spoon.

Add the mustard and continue to stir until combined.

Lightly toast the bread and place on the grill rack.

Spread the cheese mixture over the toast to cover completely.

Grill until sizzling and golden brown - this won't take long so watch carefully.

Shopping List

100g grated cheese
(Cheddar or Caerphilly)
2 tbsp beer
1 tsp wholegrain mustard
2 thick slices of bread

'Never trust a dog to watch your food'

Spanish Omelette
Serves 1 generously

Omelettes are an easy dish and quick to cook once everything is chopped. Boiled potatoes are a delicious addition, so remember, if cooking potatoes it is worth doing a few extra so that you can use them in this recipe the next day.

Shopping List

1 tbsp olive oil

1 pepper, deseeded and chopped into strips

½ courgette, chopped

1 small onion, peeled and finely chopped

If you have any boiled potatoes left over from anything, add these as well, chopped

3 eggs, beaten with a fork and seasoned

Heat the oil in a large frying pan.

Add the vegetables and cook gently for 4-5 minutes, stirring often, until softened and beginning to brown.

Add the egg mixture, keeping the heat fairly gentle and cook through. This will take just a few minutes until it is ready - too long and it will be rubbery, so keep a beady eye on it.

You may need to place the pan under the grill briefly to brown the top.

Quick and simple!

Good Old Scrambled Eggs

Serves 1

When time is short and you need a quick meal you can't beat scrambled eggs on toast and they are a really good source of protein...(protein = brain food = intelligence!).

Break the eggs into a small bowl. Add the milk and seasoning and whisk until combined.

Put the bread into the toaster and start toasting.

Put a little butter into a small saucepan (non-stick if possible) and melt over a **low** heat.

Add the egg mixture and stir continuously, keeping the heat low. The aim here is soft and creamy scrambled eggs, **not** rubbery!

Butter the toast and gently heap the egg mixture on top. Add more seasoning if required.

Shopping List

2-3 medium eggs

1 tbsp milk

Salt and pepper

2-3 slices good wholemeal bread

A little butter

'Practise safe eating – always use condiments'

Piperade
Serves 1

A recipe originally from the Basque region of Spain that is their version of scrambled eggs, definitely a different slant on the traditional variety and perfect for a tasty supper.

Shopping List

1 tbsp olive oil

1 small onion, peeled and finely chopped

1 small pepper, deseeded and chopped

1 medium tomato, roughly chopped

2 large eggs

Salt and pepper

Crusty bread or hot buttered toast, to serve

Heat the oil in a large frying pan.

Add the onion and stir-fry over a medium heat for about 5 minutes, until beginning to soften.

Add the pepper, turn the heat up and fry for another 3-4 minutes.

Remove from the heat and add the tomato.

Break the eggs into a bowl and beat lightly with a fork.

Stir the eggs into the pepper mixture. Season and return to a gentle heat, stirring until the eggs are lightly scrambled - about 2 minutes, but be careful not to overcook.

Serve immediately with crusty bread or hot buttered toast.

'Be yourself. Everyone else is already taken.' – Oscar Wilde

Lush Mushrooms on Toast

Serves 1-2

Try and find portabella mushrooms for this recipe if you can, but any good, fresh mushrooms will work just fine.

Shopping List

1 tbsp olive or vegetable oil

A good knob of butter, plus extra for spreading

1 garlic clove, crushed

450g mushrooms, chopped

Pinch of salt

Small carton of single cream

2-4 slices of bread

Chopped parsley for sprinkling on top is the finishing touch – mushrooms and parsley are such great friends, they always work well together

Put the oil and butter in a large saucepan and warm over a medium heat.

Once melted, add the garlic and fry gently for 2 minutes.

Add the mushrooms and cook gently for about 15 minutes, stirring every now and then, making sure they do not stick to the pan. The mushrooms will produce their own juice as they cook.

Add a pinch of salt and stir.

Pour in half the carton of cream. Continue to stir and cook until thickened - about 8-10 minutes. Add more cream, if needed.

Put the bread in the toaster about 3 minutes before the mushrooms are due to be ready.

Butter the toast and serve the mushrooms piled on top, with a generous sprinkling of chopped parsley.

The Ever Faithful Bacon Butty

Serves 1

The ultimate in true comfort food but it must be prepared correctly with the right ingredients and accompaniments. It's definitely worth it, there is no substitute!

Shopping List

4 rashers of back bacon
(or if using streaky, 6 rashers)

A large soft roll
(either white or brown but
it must be fresh)

Butter, for spreading

Brown or tomato sauce
(or whichever sauce is your
favourite)

Make a proper pot of tea.

Grill the bacon until it is sizzling and crispy - but watch it like a hawk.

Place on a warmed plate, cover with foil and keep warm on the floor of the grill.

Gently warm the bread roll under the grill.

Split and butter the roll.

Add the bacon and whatever sauce you fancy.

Pour a large mug of good, strong builder's tea.

Sit down and enjoy the best-ever bacon roll with a steaming mug of tea.

Absolute bliss, there is nothing better.

'Never work before breakfast; if you have to work before breakfast, eat your breakfast first.' – Josh Billings

Fish Finger Sarnies

Serves 2 – or 1 if you're very hungry

Definitely comfort food at its most childish and kitsch but absolutely irresistible – the very thought will send you speeding to the nearest grocers straight to the freezer cabinet to retrieve a pack of those glorious, golden frozen fingers.

Preheat a medium grill.

Arrange the fish fingers on the grill rack and grill for about 12-15 minutes, turning once after 6-7 minutes, until they are gorgeously golden.

Meanwhile, butter the bread and add a generous dollop of your favourite sauce to two slices.

Carefully transfer 5 cooked fish fingers onto these slices. Place the other bread slices on top of the fish fingers and press gently but firmly.

Cut diagonally (definitely tastes better) and find a cosy corner to consume.

Shopping List

Pack of 10 frozen fish fingers

4 thick slices white bread

Butter, for spreading

Tomato sauce,
salad cream or mayo
(whichever you prefer)

'Never meddle in the affairs of dragons, for you are crunchy and go well with ketchup.'

Great Big Chunky Oven Chips
Serves 1-2

These are magnificent, big stubby thick-cut chips that need very little to accompany them apart from your favourite sauce. The best thing is, they are not deep-fried but oven-cooked – a much healthier option.

Shopping List

2 medium to large potatoes, scrubbed – there's no need to peel them (Desirée are the best for chipping)

2-3 tbsp olive oil

Salt and pepper

Tomato sauce or mayonnaise

Preheat the oven to 220°C / fan oven 200°C / Gas Mark 7.

Cut the potatoes into 1cm thick sticks.

Place into a large saucepan of boiling water and boil gently for 3 minutes.

Drain the potatoes really well (they should be quite dry) then transfer to a good-sized roasting dish.

Drizzle with oil and toss the chips to coat them evenly.

Season with salt and pepper and place in the oven for about 20-25 minutes, turning the chips at least twice.

Serve with tomato sauce or mayonnaise.

'The English contribution to world cuisine – the chip' – John Cleese

'Cooking Rule: If at first you don't succeed order pizza'

Hot Dogs with Tomato & Pepper Relish

Serves 4

Everybody loves a hot dog and with this zingy relish these are just too good to resist. This recipe would also work very well if barbecuing the sausages, in which case the relish can be made in advance and simply re-heated when needed.

Shopping List

2 tbsp olive or vegetable oil

1 red onion, peeled and sliced

2 ripe tomatoes, roughly chopped

110g roasted red peppers
(from a jar), roughly chopped

1 tbsp balsamic vinegar

1 tbsp sweet chilli sauce

8 sausages

4 large rolls, warmed

Salt and pepper

Heat 1 tbsp oil in a large frying pan and gently fry the onion for 4-5 minutes until softened and beginning to brown. Remove from the pan and keep warm.

Add the remaining oil to the frying pan, add the tomatoes, peppers, balsamic vinegar and chilli sauce. Season and cook gently for 4-5 minutes until the vegetables are soft and the mixture thickens.

Meanwhile grill the sausages, turning every now and then.

Split the rolls in half, spoon the relish onto the bottom half of each roll.

Top with the sausages and fried onion and serve immediately.

'The noblest of all dogs is the hot dog; it feeds the hand that bites it.' – Lawrence J. Peter

Pitta Bread Pizzas

These are so simple and quick to make – and even easier to eat!

Preheat the grill to medium-high. Lightly toast the pitta breads on both sides.

Spread the pasta sauce on one side of the pitta breads, making sure it completely covers the surface.

Arrange the Mozzarella slices or grated Cheddar on top.

Place some tomato slices on top of the cheese, then scatter some sweetcorn on top, followed by a sprinkling of oregano and some salt and pepper.

Arrange on the grill rack and grill for 5-6 minutes until golden and bubbling. Serve and enjoy.

Shopping List

Pitta breads
(how many depends on how hungry you are)

Jar of pasta sauce
(keep the remainder in the fridge for tomorrow)

Some sliced Mozzarella cheese
(or grated Cheddar)

1-2 tomatoes, sliced

Small can sweetcorn, drained

Salt and pepper

Dried oregano
(gives that unmistakable pizza flavour)

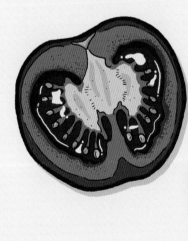

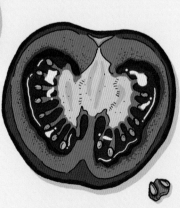

Garlic Bread

Garlic bread is the perfect accompaniment to Spaghetti Bolognese, Chilli Con Carne, Stuffed Peppers and many more dishes besides, but rather than pay the supermarket prices, why don't you make your own? It couldn't be simpler.

Shopping List

1 baguette

50g softened butter

1 garlic clove, crushed

Chopped fresh parsley is a nice addition if you have any, but not essential

Preheat the oven to 200°C / fan oven 180°C / Gas Mark 6.

Cut the baguette into thick slices, without cutting right through.

Put the butter in a bowl, add the crushed garlic and parsley (if using) and combine thoroughly with a fork.

Spread the butter mixture generously over each cut surface of the baguette.

Wrap the baguette in foil, place on baking sheet and bake for 10-15 minutes.

This will go hand in hand with any pasta dish, or just on its own.

'Garlic bread, it's the future, I've tasted it.' - Peter Kay

Bubble & Squeak

Serves 2

This is such a tasty way to use up left-over vegetables. It's so good that you may get into the habit of cooking more vegetables than you need in order to wind up with a surplus!

Shopping List

500g cooked potatoes, mashed

250g cooked cabbage or spring greens

25g softened butter

2-3 spring onions, chopped finely

Salt and pepper

A little flour

Some vegetable oil for frying

Combine the mashed potatoes with the cabbage or spring greens. Add the butter, spring onions and some seasoning, mixing well with a fork.

Divide the mixture into eight and shape into round balls, then flatten them gently between your hands. Dip your hands into cold water if the mixture sticks to you.

Toss the patties in a bowl of flour to coat them, then place on a plate.

Chill in the fridge for at least 40 minutes.

Heat 1cm of vegetable oil in a frying-pan. Once hot, carefully lower in the patties using a fish slice.

Cook them for about 3-4 minutes on each side, until golden brown and crispy.

Serve with bacon or on their own as a fabulous savoury treat.

'Knock Hard, Ring Loud, Life is Deaf!'

Jacket Potatoes

This has got to be one of the best ways of eating potatoes. It's easy to ring the changes with different fillings – yet so simple.

Preheat the oven to 220°C / fan oven 200°C / Gas Mark 7.

Scrub and dry the potatoes with a cloth.

Prick the potatoes in several places with a fork.

To give a crisp tasty skin, rub the potatoes with a little olive oil and salt.

Place the potatoes directly on the oven shelf towards the top of the oven. Large potatoes will take 1-1½ hours to bake, test with a sharp knife to see if they are cooked.

Once cooked, slit the potatoes open and serve with a knob of butter and a generous helping of grated cheese.

If you feel like being more adventurous, the perfect partner for these potatoes is 'Wonderful Waldorf Salad' on page 32. If time is short or you are feeling less than energetic, you can't go wrong with a can of baked beans.

Shopping List

1-2 medium sized potatoes
– King Edwards, Maris Piper and Desirée potatoes will all work well

Olive oil

Salt

Butter

Grated cheese

Quick Chicken Noodles

Serves 2

Although this recipe is in the 'Quick Bites' section, it is definitely more of a substantial snack. It's so tasty and great if you have some left over chicken that needs using.

Shopping List

2 nests of dried egg noodles

1 tsp cornflour
(great for thickening sauces)

250ml chicken stock
(use a stock cube)

1 tbsp dark soy sauce

100g cooked chicken, shredded

50g frozen sweetcorn

75g frozen peas

2 spring onions, finely sliced

1. Cook the noodles according to pack instructions. Drain and keep warm.

2. In a cup, mix the cornflour with 2 tsp of cold water until blended.

3. Put the stock into a saucepan with the soy sauce, chicken, sweetcorn and peas. Bring to simmering point and simmer gently for 2-3 minutes.

4. Add the blended cornflour and stir until the mixture thickens.

5. Add the noodles and spring onions, continuing to warm through for a further 2 minutes.

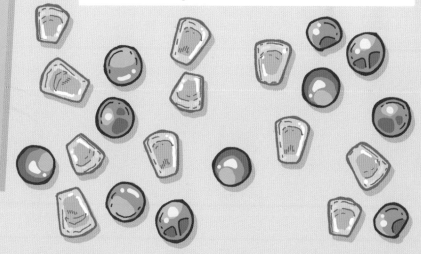

Speedy Tuna Pasta

Serves 1-2

Always try and keep canned tuna in your store cupboard – it's so versatile. In this recipe it transforms ordinary pasta into a tasty dish that will satisfy any case of the munchies. Freshly snipped parsley added before serving makes this dish and is great for scattering over vegetables and salads, so it's worthwhile buying a pot from the supermarket to keep on your window sill.

Shopping List

1 tbsp olive oil

1 garlic clove, crushed

1 small (200g) can tuna, drained and flaked

1 tbsp tomato purée

400g can chopped tomatoes

2 tbsp chopped fresh parsley, plus extra to garnish

Salt and pepper

100g pasta (tagliatelle or spaghetti works best)

Heat the oil in a pan, add the garlic and fry gently for 2-3 minutes, but be careful that it doesn't burn.

Add the drained tuna and tomato purée and stir gently for 2 minutes.

Add the tomatoes, parsley and some seasoning and simmer gently for 15-20 minutes until the sauce has reduced, giving an occasional stir.

Meanwhile, cook the pasta according to instructions.

Drain the pasta, return to pan and add the tuna mixture to this, stirring gently but thoroughly.

Serve immediately with a generous scattering of fresh parsley.

Corned Beef Hash

Serves 4

This is a hearty, warming dish which is good on its own but can be served with carrots or cabbage if you want to make it more of a main meal. Delicious whichever way it's served and sure to become a definite favourite.

Shopping List

5-6 medium potatoes, peeled and diced into large cubes

2 tbsp olive oil

2 medium onions, peeled and sliced

340g can corned beef, diced

Worcester sauce

Salt and pepper

Some freshly snipped parsley from your window sill

Cook the potatoes in boiling water for 5-6 minutes until just tender. Drain.

Heat the oil in a large frying pan. Add the onions and fry over a medium heat for 4-5 minutes, stirring often.

Once the onions are beginning to brown, add the potatoes and cook for 3-4 minutes.

Add the corned beef and a generous splash of Worcester sauce. Season with salt and pepper. Spread the mixture evenly over the pan and press down gently with a metal fish slice.

Cook over a medium heat for 5-6 minutes, which will allow the under-side to become crispy, but do not stir.

Carefully turn the mixture over and continue to cook for 5 minutes without stirring. The object is to finish with lots of lovely tasty crispy bits throughout the mixture.

Serve with a generous scattering of snipped parsley.

'If opportunity doesn't knock build a door'

Wonderful Waldorf Salad

Serves 2-3

A really good substantial salad that was originally created at New York's Waldorf-Astoria Hotel in the 1890's and is the perfect partner to a baked potato. The apple and celery add a terrific fulfilling crunch and the addition of Greek yoghurt makes a delicious light dressing.

Shopping List

½ small onion, diced

2 sticks celery, finely sliced (the remainder can be used in a stir-fry or Bolognese)

1 eating apple, cored and chopped (it's hard to beat the crispness of an English Cox)

40g walnut pieces, chopped

A small handful of raisins

1 tbsp mayonnaise

3 tbsp Greek yoghurt

Salt and pepper

Mix together the onion, celery, apple, half the walnuts, raisins, mayonnaise and Greek yoghurt. Season with a little salt and pepper. Place in the coolest part of the fridge (i.e. towards the bottom) for at least 30 minutes, to allow the flavours to fuse.

Serve chilled, with the remaining walnuts sprinkled on top.

You will have some walnuts left over and these can be put to good use in the heavenly Coffee and Walnut Cake recipe on page 88.

'Vegetarian: an old Indian word for bad hunter' – Anon

Warm Potato, Green Bean & Cherry Tomato Salad

Serves 2

This magnificent salad can be put together quickly to provide a satisfying snack to keep those hunger pangs at bay.

Shopping List

Small pack of baby new potatoes, halved

Generous pinch of salt

200g fine green beans, trimmed

Cherry tomatoes (use as many as you wish), halved

Basil leaves

Olive oil

Pesto sauce

Cook the potatoes in a saucepan of boiling, salted water for 15 minutes, adding the green beans for the final 5 minutes to cook until just tender. Drain well, place in a salad bowl and allow to cool for approximately 10 minutes.

Add the cherry tomatoes to the potatoes and beans.

Tear in some basil leaves and add a generous tablespoon of pesto sauce. Drizzle with olive oil.

Mix everything together gently so that all the ingredients are lightly coated and combined - but not mashed!

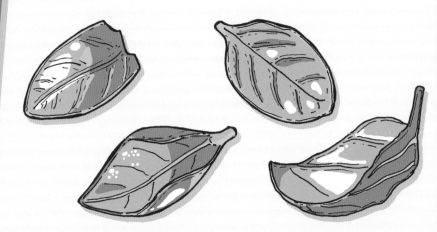

'Don't offer me advice. Give me money.'

Proper
Main
Meals

The Full-on Fry-up
Easy Chicken Curry
Perfect Prawn Curry
Simple Thai Green Curry
Chilli Con Carne
Chicken & Rice in a Pot
Chipolatas with Cherry Tomatoes
Lemon & Chicken Risotto
Pasta with Peas & Ham
Pasta with Tasty Tomato Sauce
Bolognese
Vegetarian Bolognese
Pasta Bake
Pan Haggerty
Simple Sausage & Potato Casserole
Vegetable Casserole
Wheeler's Beef Stew & Dumplings
Sticky Onion Marmalade Sausages
Mash
Pan-Fried Gammon
Roast Chicken
Roast Potatoes
Chicken Soup
Potato & Roots Hash
Cauliflower Cheese
Stuffed Peppers

The Full-on Fry-up

As much a part of Britain as cups of tea, castles and custard, the fry-up is part of our heritage but it takes a little bit of preparation in order to serve everything at the same time and, of course, hot.

Shopping List (per person)

2 sausages

Butter and vegetable oil

2–3 medium mushrooms, wiped clean and chopped

2–3 rashers of back bacon, 3–4 if streaky

½ 400g can of baked beans

1 medium tomato, sliced

2 slices of bread

1 large egg

Heat the oven to 130°C / fan oven 110°C / Gas Mark ½ and put plates in to warm. Also place a baking sheet or serving plate in the oven to keep things warm as they cook.

Preheat the grill to moderate. Grill the sausages, turning occasionally so that they cook evenly. They should take about 15 minutes to cook.

Melt a knob of butter in a small saucepan and add the mushrooms. Cook over a gentle heat, stirring every now and then.

Place the bacon next to the sausages under the grill. It won't take very long to cook but once it is done it will happily keep warm in the oven with the sausages.

Heat the beans very gently in a saucepan.

Heat a little oil in a frying pan until sizzling and then add the tomatoes. Cook gently and turn over, being careful not to break the slices up. Once ready, transfer to the serving plate or baking sheet in the oven.

Place bread into the toaster.

Add a little oil to the frying pan. Break the egg onto a saucer. Once the oil is sizzling carefully slide in the egg. Cook gently to your liking, spooning a little of the hot oil over the egg to set the surface.

Once everything is cooked, serve on a warm plate with a dollop of your favourite sauce.

Easy Chicken Curry

Serves 4 – so easy to share

This is a wonderfully easy recipe for a chicken curry. Make it as hot or as mild as you like, depending on what strength curry powder you use. Naan bread is a perfect partner for this dish, so stock up in the supermarket.

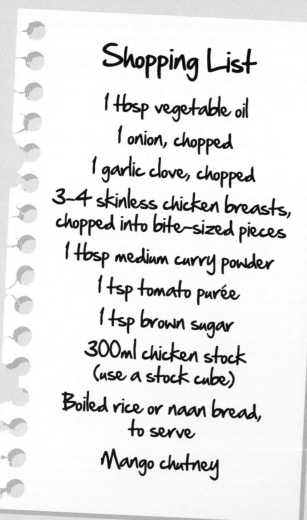

Shopping List

1 tbsp vegetable oil

1 onion, chopped

1 garlic clove, chopped

3–4 skinless chicken breasts, chopped into bite-sized pieces

1 tbsp medium curry powder

1 tsp tomato purée

1 tsp brown sugar

300ml chicken stock (use a stock cube)

Boiled rice or naan bread, to serve

Mango chutney

A good-sized shallow pan with a lid is ideal for this but an ordinary saucepan will be fine.

Heat the oil in a large shallow pan or saucepan. Add the onion and garlic and fry gently for 3-4 minutes, until softened.

Add the chicken and fry gently for a further 3-4 minutes.

Stir in the curry powder, tomato purée and sugar, gently mixing together.

Pour in the chicken stock, give one last stir and bring to the boil. Reduce to a gentle heat, then cover and cook for 40 minutes.

Serve with boiled rice or naan bread (or both) and don't forget the mango chutney.

Perfect Prawn Carry

Serves 2

A great recipe for a speedy curry that will provide a tasty supper when time is short.

Shopping List

1 tbsp vegetable oil

1 medium onion, finely chopped

1 garlic clove, crushed

2 tbsp curry paste
(if you like your curry hot
add 1 extra tbsp)

200g cooked peeled prawns
(look in the supermarket for the
value packs on fresh
fish shelves)

400g can chopped tomatoes

Salt and pepper

Small handful fresh coriander,
chopped

Naan bread and boiled rice,
to serve

Gently heat the oil in a frying pan or wok. Add the onion and garlic, stirring over a low heat for about 3-4 minutes.

Add the curry paste and cook for 2-3 more minutes.

Add the prawns and tomatoes and bring to a gentle simmer.

Cook gently for 7-8 minutes, season and then add the coriander.

Serve with naan bread and boiled rice.

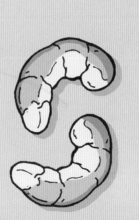
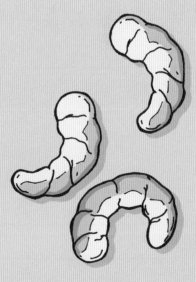

Simple Thai Green Curry

Serves 1

A favourite tasty Thai curry recipe that is good enough to share with friends and is bound to impress. Just increase the quantities to suit your needs.

Shopping List

1 tbsp olive oil

1 skinless chicken breast, chopped into bite-sized pieces

1 small onion, chopped

1 garlic clove, crushed

1 tbsp Thai green curry paste

1 tbsp Greek yoghurt

½ can coconut milk

50g frozen peas

100g basmati rice

½ lemon

Some freshly snipped coriander

Heat the olive oil in a wok or saucepan and add the chicken, onion and garlic, cooking over a medium-high heat for 2-3 minutes until lightly browned.

Stir in the curry paste, yoghurt and coconut milk and finally the peas.

Bring to the boil, then reduce the heat to a simmer. Cook for a further 12-15 minutes.

Meanwhile, cook the rice according to pack instructions.

Squeeze the lemon juice over the curry and add the coriander, giving everything a good stir. Cook for a further 2 minutes.

Serve with fluffy basmati rice.

'Hunger is the best pickle' - Benjamin Franklin

'Laugh Often, Dream Big and Reach for the Stars'

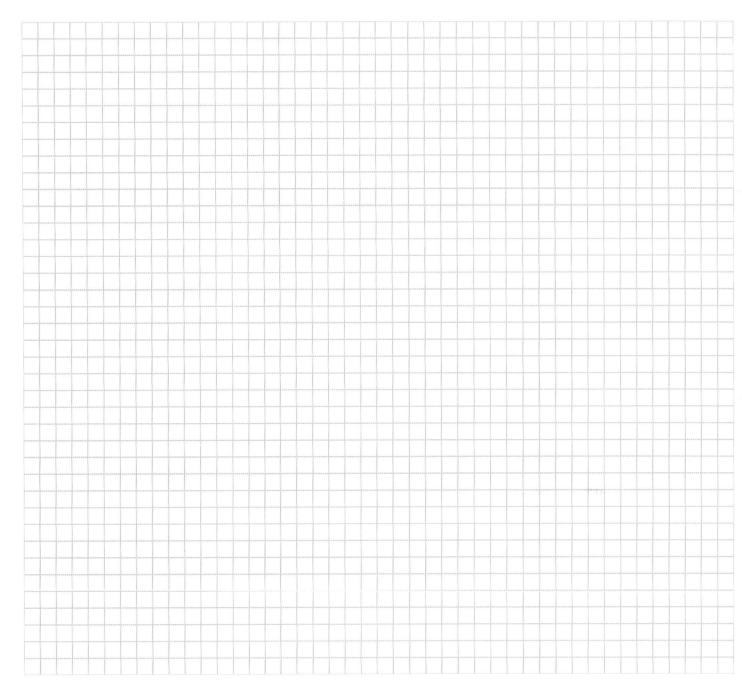

Chilli Con Carne

Serves 4

This should be on every student's agenda – it goes down well with everyone and it's great for a get-together with friends. Even better, it doesn't cost the earth.

Shopping List

500g minced beef

1 large onion, chopped

1 garlic clove, crushed

400g can chopped tomatoes

400g can kidney beans in chilli sauce

1/2 tsp chilli powder

A dash of Worcestershire sauce

Salt and pepper

Boiled rice or garlic bread, to serve

Heat a large saucepan and add the minced beef, a handful at a time, so that it sears and browns, breaking up the mince with a wooden spoon. This browning will give the chilli a great flavour.

Add the onion and garlic and continue to cook for a further 3-4 minutes, until the onion has softened.

Add the tomatoes, kidney beans, chilli powder and Worcestershire sauce. Season with a little salt and pepper. Mix thoroughly and bring to the boil.

Reduce the heat and simmer gently with a lid on for 25-30 minutes. Check and stir from time to time, adding a splash of water, if needed.

Remove the lid, taste to see if further seasoning is required (the can of chilli beans is usually pre-seasoned so you may only need a little more, if any). If the sauce needs to be thicker, turn up the heat a little and continue to cook without the lid for further 10 minutes or so until the sauce has reduced and is rich and thick.

Serve with boiled rice or garlic bread.

Chicken & Rice in a Pot

Serves 2-3

This is a fabulous one-pot dish that you can prepare and leave to cook happily on a low heat – so straightforward and delicious.

Shopping List

1 tbsp vegetable oil

1 medium onion

6 chicken drumsticks

175g long grain rice

600ml chicken stock
(use a stock cube)

3 carrots, peeled and cut
into small chunks

Salt and pepper

Heat the oil in a large saucepan and fry the onion gently for 3-4 minutes.

Add the chicken drumsticks and fry until lightly browned on all sides.

Add the rice and cook for 2 minutes, stirring continuously.

Pour in the stock and add the carrots. Season with salt and pepper.

Simmer gently, covered, for 40-45 minutes until the chicken is tender.

Go on...dig in.

'I like rice. Rice is great if you're hungry and you want 2000 of something.' – Mitch Hedberg

Chipolatas with Cherry Toms
Serves 3-4

This goes very well with pasta, rice or a crusty baguette and it's easy to double up if you want to cook for a few friends.

Shopping List

Pack of chipolata sausages

1 tbsp olive oil

A punnet of cherry tomatoes (look for the cheap 'value' punnets in supermarkets)

2 cups of frozen peas or 1 cup of peas, 1 cup frozen sweetcorn

Salt and pepper

Chopped fresh parsley (if you have any)

Preheat the oven to 180°C / fan oven 160°C / Gas Mark 4.

Cut the chipolatas in half and place them in a roasting pan. Drizzle with a little olive oil and transfer to the oven to cook for 15 minutes.

Add the cherry tomatoes, frozen peas and/or sweetcorn. Season with a little salt and pepper.

Cook for a further 15 minutes, then scatter some parsley over if you have any. Serve with pasta, rice or a crusty baguette.

Lemon & Chicken Risotto

Serves 2

A wonderfully simple risotto and with the addition of some grated Parmesan or Cheddar when serving, it is better still. Don't be tempted to rush this recipe, the stock needs to be added gradually and absorbed before adding the next lot, but the result is well worth the effort.

Shopping List

1 lemon
225g chicken strips
1 tbsp olive oil
1 garlic clove, crushed
280g risotto rice
750ml hot chicken stock (use 2 stock cubes)
100g frozen peas

Preheat the oven to 200°C / fan oven 180°C / Gas Mark 6.

Finely grate the lemon zest from the lemon (this is the yellow part of the skin – avoid the white part, which has a bitter taste).

Cut the lemon in half and squeeze the juice into a cup.

Put the chicken strips into an ovenproof dish, pour the lemon juice and zest over them and cook in the oven for 20 minutes.

Meanwhile, heat the oil in a pan and fry the garlic gently for 1-2 minutes, stirring so it doesn't stick to the pan.

Add the rice and stir well to coat the rice with the oil and garlic.

Gradually add the stock to the rice with a ladle, making sure each lot is absorbed before adding the next.

Add the frozen peas once half the stock has been added.

Once all the stock is absorbed, add the chicken strips and stir thoroughly.

'Chaos, panic, pandemonium – my work here is done'

Pasta with Peas & Ham

Serves 2

Pasta is so useful and always provides a great tasty meal. It is an essential store cupboard item that is versatile and can be made into hundreds of tasty dishes.

Shopping List

150-160g tagliatelle
(or any other pasta)

50g butter

1 medium onion, peeled and thinly sliced

50g cooked ham, chopped

50g frozen peas

2 tbsp single cream

50g grated Cheddar cheese

Salt and pepper

Cook the pasta in boiling salted water for about 10 minutes until tender, but not soft.

Meanwhile, heat the butter in a frying pan, add the onion and cook for about 3-4 minutes, until soft.

Add the ham and peas and cook for a further 5 minutes, stirring often.

Drain the pasta and return it to the saucepan. Add the ham mixture, then gently stir in the cream and most of the cheese.

Season and serve immediately, sprinkled with the remaining cheese. Snip some fresh parsley on the top if you have any.

Pasta with Tasty Tomato Sauce

Serves 2

A simple dish to make that is delicious, requires very little effort and provides that classic combination of tomatoes and pasta. Any extras you want to add are up to you – the only limit is your imagination!

Shopping List

2 tbsp olive oil

1 medium onion, chopped

1 stick celery, chopped

1 large garlic clove, crushed

400g can chopped tomatoes

225g pasta shapes

Finely grated Parmesan or hard goat's cheese
(which has a more mellow flavour)

Salt and pepper

Heat 1 tbsp olive oil in a large frying pan.

Add the onion, celery and garlic and cook gently until softened - about 6-7 minutes.

Add the tomatoes, stirring well. Continue to cook, reducing to a lovely thick sauce, about 7-8 minutes.

Meanwhile, put the pasta into a large saucepan of boiling salted water and reduce to a simmer. See pack instructions for cooking time.

Drain the pasta and return it to the warm saucepan.

Drizzle the remaining olive oil into the pasta.

Gently stir the tomato mixture into the pasta. Season.

Serve and sprinkle generously with the Parmesan or goat's cheese.

Bolognese
Serves 3-4

Everybody has their own particular version of this dish but this recipe is straightforward and can be used for the basis of many different dishes.

Shopping List

1 tbsp vegetable oil

1/2 medium onion, (or 1 small onion) chopped

1 stick celery, chopped

1 garlic clove, crushed

225g minced beef

A generous splodge of tomato purée

400g can chopped tomatoes

150ml beef stock (use a stock cube)

Salt and pepper

Pasta to accompany

Finely grated Parmesan or hard goat's cheese, to serve

Heat the oil in a large saucepan and gently fry the onion, celery and garlic for 3-4 minutes until beginning to colour and soften.

Add the mince, breaking it up gently so that it begins to brown. If necessary, spoon off some of the excess fat that has been produced.

Add the tomato purée, tomatoes, stock and seasoning. Stir well.

Put a lid on the saucepan and bring to the boil, then lower heat and simmer gently for 30 minutes.

Put the pasta on to cook in plenty of boiling, salted water. Leave the lid off whilst it cooks for 10-12 minutes, until tender.

At the same time, remove the lid from the Bolognese and turn the heat up slightly to reduce the liquid to make a nice thick sauce.

Once everything is ready, drain the pasta and serve with a generous helping of Bolognese and of course, some grated Parmesan or hard goat's cheese.

Vegetarian Bolognese
Serves 2-3

This is a versatile and really useful sauce that can be served with pasta as a filling and nutritious meal. You can easily double up the amounts below to make an inexpensive dinner for 6.

Shopping List

1 tbsp olive oil

1 small onion, chopped

1 garlic clove, crushed

1 carrot, grated

1 celery stick, sliced

400g can chopped tomatoes

A generous splodge of tomato purée

60g dried red lentils, rinsed

220ml vegetable stock

Salt and pepper

Heat the olive oil in a saucepan and gently fry the onion, garlic, carrot and celery for approximately 6-7 minutes, until soft.

Add the tomatoes, tomato purée, lentils, stock, salt and pepper. Bring the mixture to the boil, then partially cover with a lid and simmer gently for 20-25 minutes until the Bolognese has thickened.

Serve with pasta for a satisfying, nutritious meal.

'Life is a combination of magic and pasta' – Federico Fellini

'Always be sincere, even if you don't mean it' - Harry S. Truman

Pasta Bake
Serves 2

This delicious wintry pasta dish really ticks all the boxes – minimal preparation and the perfect fusion of cheese and pasta. Result – a cheery, warming, savoury treat!

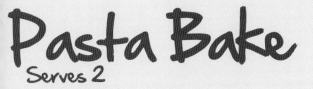

Shopping List

1 tbsp olive oil

2 medium garlic cloves, crushed

220g leeks, washed and sliced very finely
(then rinse again in a colander)

2 medium eggs

75ml single cream

75g grated Cheddar cheese

50g cooked pasta shells, penne or fusilli

Salt and pepper

Preheat the oven to 180°C / fan oven 160°C / Gas Mark 4.

Heat the oil in a frying pan and add the garlic and leeks, cooking them gently for about 5 minutes until soft.

Beat the eggs and cream in a large bowl and add the cheese and cooked pasta.

Add the cooked leeks to the pasta mixture. Season and combine gently.

Transfer to a lightly greased ovenproof dish.

Bake for about 25 minutes. The egg mixture should be set and golden brown.

'All you see I owe to spaghetti.' – Sophia Loren

Pan Haggerty

Serves 2-3

This amazingly colourful dish looks so comforting when it comes out of the oven – everybody will want some!

Shopping List

Butter or olive oil, for greasing

1 small onion, sliced

450g potatoes, peeled and thinly sliced

100g Red Leicester cheese, grated

150ml milk

150ml single cream

Salt and pepper

Preheat the oven to 180°C / fan oven 160°C / Gas Mark 4.

Lightly grease an ovenproof dish with butter or olive oil.

Layer the onion, potatoes and cheese, keeping aside some cheese for the topping.

Mix together the milk and cream, seasoning lightly with salt and pepper.

Pour the milk and cream over the layered potato mixture. Sprinkle with the remaining cheese and bake for about 35-40 minutes.

Goes well with grilled bacon – or anything you fancy really!

Simple Sausage & Potato Casserole

Serves 4

This is such an easy dish to rustle up and will deliver a satisfying meal that is packed with flavour.

Shopping List

1 tbsp olive or vegetable oil

500g small new potatoes, scrubbed and halved

454g pack sausages, chopped into bite-sized pieces

1 onion, chopped finely

1 green pepper, deseeded and diced

340g jar tomato pasta sauce

Heat the oil in large frying pan and fry the potatoes and sausages for 10 minutes, stirring often.

Add the onion and pepper and cook for further 5 minutes, turning the sausages until browned.

Add the pasta sauce, rinse the jar with a splash of water and add to the pan. Cover and cook for further 15 minutes.

Hey presto, it's ready.

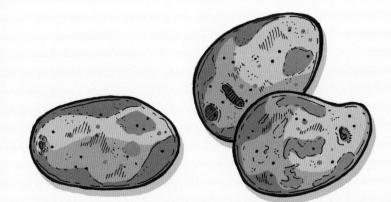

Vegetable Casserole
Serves 2

This dish requires a little bit of preparation, mainly peeling, but it's well worth the effort. It's a great warming meal that is bound to be a winner during winter months.

Shopping List

2 tbsp olive oil

2 onions, peeled and sliced

450g potatoes, peeled and chopped

1 large carrot, peeled and chopped

1 courgette, sliced

100g cabbage, chopped finely

400g can red kidney beans, drained and rinsed

110g frozen peas

450ml vegetable stock (use a stock cube)

1 tbsp tomato purée

Preheat the oven to 200°C / fan oven 180°C / Gas Mark 6.

Heat the oil in a frying pan and add the onions, potatoes and carrot. Cook gently, stirring often, for 10 minutes.

Place this mixture in a casserole dish with the courgette, cabbage, beans and peas.

Add the stock to the casserole with the tomato purée. Season.

Bake for 30-40 minutes.

Serve with triangles of toast.

'Everybody makes mistakes. The trick is to make mistakes when nobody is looking.'

Wheeler's Beef Stew & Dumplings

Serves 4

This is a nourishing and filling beef stew that everyone will love. Mr Wheeler is passionate about good, simple fare and this timeless classic has been handed down through the Wheeler generations.

Shopping List

1 tbsp vegetable oil

450g braising beef, cubed

1 medium onion, chopped

1 small swede, diced

1 parsnip, diced

2 carrots, diced

500ml beef stock
(use a stock cube)

Salt and pepper

2 tbsp cornflour

For the dumplings

110g self-raising flour

50g shredded beef suet

Salt and pepper

Heat the oil in a large saucepan and add the beef and onion. Cook, stirring continuously, until nicely browned.

Add the diced vegetables and continue to stir well.

Add the stock and seasoning. Bring to the boil, then reduce the heat to a gentle simmer. Cook for about 90 minutes, until the meat is tender.

To make the dumplings, combine the flour, suet, salt and pepper in a bowl. Add a little water - but not too much - to make a soft, but not sticky, dough. Shape into 8 dumplings, then cover and set aside.

About 20 minutes before the stew is due to be served, blend the cornflour with 3 tbsp cold water and add to the stew, stirring until thickened.

Add the dumplings, then cover and simmer gently for 20 minutes until they are light and fluffy.

Serve with fresh, crusty bread.

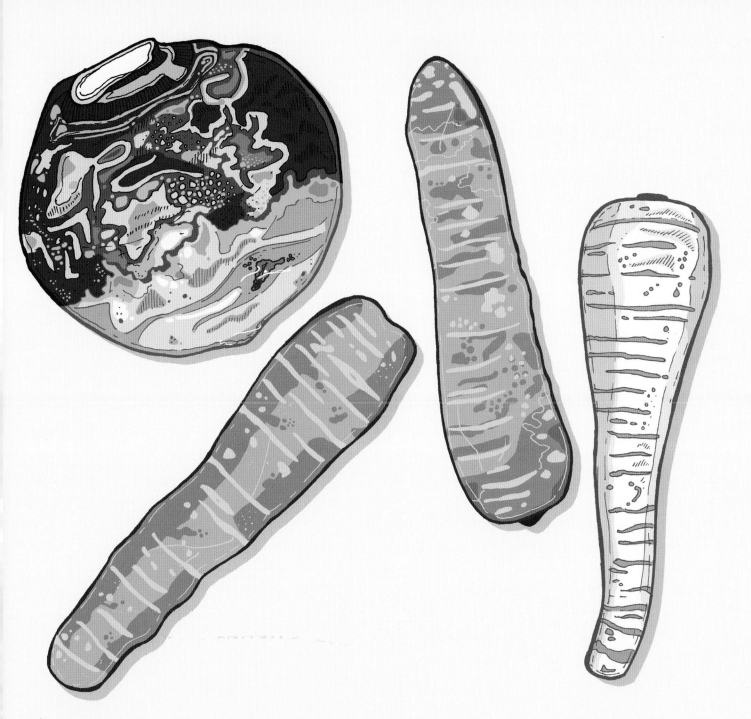

'Talk of joy: There may be better things than beef stew and baked potatoes and home-
made bread... there may be.' – David Grayson

Sticky Onion Marmalade Sausages

Serves 3-4

Onion marmalade is a really useful store cupboard item. It makes a cheese sandwich superb and it gives the sausages in this recipe a heavenly sticky glaze. The perfect partner has to be mash.

Shopping List

8 sausages

4 tbsp onion marmalade

Preheat the oven to 190°C / fan oven 170°C / Gas Mark 5.

Put the sausages into a roasting tin and cook in the oven until browned, approximately 35-40 minutes.

Drain off the fat and spoon the onion marmalade on top.

Return to the oven and cook for approximately 8 more minutes.

Love and sausages are alike. Can never have enough of either. – Trixie Koontz

Mash

Potatoes such as Maris Piper or Desirée are ideal and produce a perfect fluffy mash.
Allow about 2 per person or 1 if they are large.

Wash and peel the potatoes.

Cut into even sized chunks.

Place into a pan and cover with cold water with a pinch of salt. Cover the pan and bring to the boil.

Reduce the heat and simmer for about 20 minutes or until tender, test with a knife.

Drain the potatoes in a colander and return to the pan.

Add a generous knob of butter and some black pepper. Mash vigorously!

Serve with whatever you wish, but Sticky Onion Marmalade Sausages are hard to beat.

Shopping List

Maris Piper or
Desirée potatoes

Knob of butter

Salt and pepper

Pan-fried Gammon
Serves 2

This is another really good partner to the mash and perfect when you want something a little bit special but still very simple to do.

Snip the rind on the gammon steaks to stop them curling up.

Heat the oil in a frying pan and add the steaks, cooking them for about 5 minutes on each side.

Add the cider and allow to boil for 2 minutes.

Reduce the heat to a simmer.

Add the cream, stirring continuously and cook for about 3 minutes until thickened.

Season and serve with fluffy mashed potatoes.

Comforting and tasty...

Shopping List

2 gammon steaks
1 tbsp olive oil
125ml dry cider
2 tbsp double cream

'Slicing a warm slab of bacon is a lot like giving a ferret a shave. No matter how careful you are, somebody's going to get hurt.' – Alton Brown

'Food for thought is no substitute for the real thing.' – Walt Kelly

Roast Chicken

Who doesn't love the heavenly smell of a chicken roasting? It's bound to set the taste buds tingling so get together with some friends and do a traditional roast.

Preheat the oven to 180°C / fan oven 160°C / Gas Mark 4.

Put the chicken into a roasting pan. Rub the butter over the skin of the chicken and sprinkle with some salt and pepper.

Cut the lemon in half and push it into the cavity of the chicken to give it a lovely lemony hint. Roast for 1 ½ - 1 ¾ hours until cooked. To test whether the bird is cooked, make sure the juices are clear by sticking a skewer into the thigh. If the juices are pinkish, place the chicken back into the oven and repeat the juice test every 15 minutes until they are clear.

When cooked, place onto a warm serving plate and leave to rest until ready to carve.

Shopping List

1 largish chicken
1.5kg-2.25kg
at room temperature
(make sure it has been out of
the fridge for at least 2 hours)

Knob of butter

Salt and pepper

1 lemon

Roast Potatoes
Serves 4

The secret with good roast potatoes is to partly boil (parboil) them first so that you can drain them and then whilst still in the pan, shake like fury to bash the edges!

Preheat the oven to 220°C / fan oven 200°C / Gas Mark 7.

Place potatoes in salted boiling water and boil for 10 minutes.

Drain and shake the pan vigorously to roughen the potatoes. Transfer to a roasting tin.

Drizzle olive oil over the potatoes to coat them lightly but thoroughly.

Roast in the top of the oven for approximately 45 minutes, turning twice until they are golden brown.

Shopping List

About 8 large potatoes (Desiree, King Edward or Maris Piper), peeled and halved

Olive oil

Salt

Chicken Soup

Makes about 2 litres

After you have roasted a chicken you can use the carcass to make a delicious soup which is full of flavour and really good for warding off winter chills and colds.

Place chicken carcass in a large saucepan. Add the onion, carrot and about 1 ½ litres water (you will need a container large enough to store this in the fridge). Season with salt and pepper. Bring to the boil.

Reduce heat and simmer for 2 hours.

Strain the liquid through a large sieve or colander, discarding the carcass, onion and carrot. This is your stock; it can be stored in the fridge for 3-4 days until needed.

Shopping List

For the stock

Chicken carcass

1/2 onion, peeled

1 carrot, peeled and chopped into large chunks

Salt and pepper

For the soup

(You can add stuff or leave stuff out depending on what you have got, adding any vegetables that need using up)

40g butter

2-3 potatoes, peeled and chopped

2-3 carrots, peeled and chopped

1 onion or leek, peeled and chopped

½ turnip, peeled and chopped

1-2 stalks celery, chopped

A few cabbage leaves, chopped

Handful of spaghetti

To make the soup

Melt the butter in a large saucepan on a gentle heat. Add the chopped vegetables, place the lid on the saucepan and let the vegetables 'sweat' for about half an hour on a very gentle heat.

Next add the stock, bring the soup to the boil, then reduce the heat and simmer for about 30 minutes.

Liquidise the soup (a hand blender is easiest if you have one, or remove some of the vegetables with a slotted spoon and mash roughly with a fork, return to soup and stir thoroughly).

Snap the spaghetti into short lengths, add to the soup and simmer for about 10 minutes to cook the pasta (refer to cooking times on pasta pack).

'Cooking is like love. It should be entered into with abandon or not at all.' – Harriet van Horne

Potato & Roots Hash

Serves 3-4

A perfect chum for sausages, chicken or whatever floats your boat.

Shopping List

500ml vegetable stock
(use a stock cube)

3 potatoes,
peeled and chopped

3 carrots,
peeled and chopped

1 turnip,
peeled and chopped

15g butter,
cut into small pieces

Salt and pepper

Preheat the oven to 190°C / fan oven 170°C / Gas Mark 5.

Pour the stock into a large saucepan and add the vegetables.

Bring to the boil, then cover and simmer gently for approximately 25 minutes.

Pour off the excess stock.

Season with salt and pepper and mash the vegetables until smooth.

Place into an ovenproof dish and dot the surface with small chunks of butter.

Cook for approximately 15-20 minutes until golden brown.

Really good with sausages or chicken.

'I'm sick of following my dreams. I'm just going to ask them where they are going and hook up with them later.' – Mitch Hedberg

Cauliflower Cheese

Serves 2

A classic old school favourite that everyone remembers from their childhood. In this recipe you will master a basic cheese sauce, which is really simple to make and so useful as a base for many other dishes.

Shopping List

1 medium cauliflower

25g butter

25g cornflour
(this is really good for thickening or making sauces)

300ml milk

75g grated Cheddar cheese
(or more if you like a really cheesy sauce)

Crusty bread, to serve

Preheat the oven to 190°C / fan oven 170°C / Gas Mark 5.

Break the cauliflower into florets and add to a pan of salted boiling water. Cook over a moderate heat for about 6 minutes or until just tender.

Drain the cauliflower and place in an ovenproof dish or casserole.

Melt the butter in a saucepan.

Remove from the heat and add the cornflour, mixing to a smooth paste.

Add a little milk and stir. Place back on a moderate heat and gradually add the rest of the milk, stirring gently all the time.

Bring to the boil, stirring continuously, then reduce the heat and simmer for about 1-2 minutes, still stirring, until thickened.

Add the cheese and a little seasoning and stir until the cheese has melted.

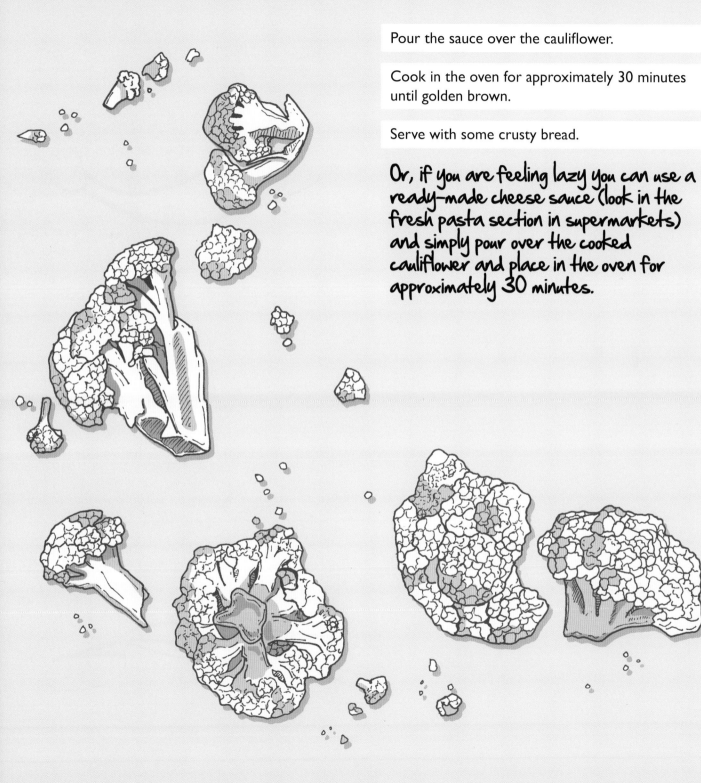

Pour the sauce over the cauliflower.

Cook in the oven for approximately 30 minutes until golden brown.

Serve with some crusty bread.

Or, if you are feeling lazy you can use a ready-made cheese sauce (look in the fresh pasta section in supermarkets) and simply pour over the cooked cauliflower and place in the oven for approximately 30 minutes.

Stuffed Peppers

Serves 4

One pepper per person is ample, there is usually some extra filling that can be cooked alongside the peppers and it is a surprisingly filling meal served with good crusty bread.

Shopping List

4 peppers

1 tbsp oil

1 onion, chopped

1 large garlic clove, crushed

Approx. 6 fresh mint leaves, chopped

½ tsp ground cinnamon

225g minced beef or lamb

400g can chopped tomatoes

110g long grain rice

275ml beef stock (use a stock cube)

Crusty bread, to serve

Preheat the oven to 190°C / fan oven 170°C / Gas Mark 5.

Cut the tops off the peppers and put them to one side. Remove the seeds from the inside of each pepper and carefully trim the base so that the pepper stands upright and does not wobble. Arrange in a shallow ovenproof dish.

Heat the oil in a frying pan. Add the onion, garlic, mint and cinnamon and cook gently for about 4 minutes.

Add the mince, stirring until browned.

Stir in the remaining ingredients, bring to the boil, then lower the heat and simmer for 10 minutes until the rice is half cooked and the liquid is almost absorbed.

Fill the peppers with the mince and rice mixture, then replace the tops. Any extra mixture may be cooked alongside the peppers.

Cover the dish loosely with foil and bake for about 40 minutes. Serve with some crusty bread.

'Heard there was a party. Came.' – Beatrice Lillie

Biscuits,
Puddings
&
Cakes

Pancakes!
Fab Fruity Flapjacks
No-Bake Fridge Cake
Fat Rascals
Jumbles
Bread & Butter Pudding
Baked Bananas
Coffee & Walnut Cake
Carrot Cake
Raspberry Muffins

Pancakes!
Should make about 5-6

Make these pancakes whenever you feel like a treat – for breakfast, a mid afternoon snack or when those evening hunger pangs strike. Don't forget to allow time for the batter to rest before cooking.

Shopping List

125g plain flour

Pinch of salt

1 large egg

300ml milk

Knob of butter

Lemon juice and sugar, to serve

Sift the flour and the salt into a mixing bowl.

Make a well in the centre, add the egg and milk and whisk well, incorporating the flour until the mixture is batter-like. Set aside for 1 hour or so.

Put a knob of butter into a frying pan to lubricate the pan and gently heat, then pour off any excess butter and add 2-3 tbsp of batter to the pan, tilting the pan to spread the batter.

It will cook very quickly so watch carefully, lifting the edges with a knife to see if it is golden underneath. If it is, flip the pancake over and cook very briefly on the other side.

Once cooked, slide onto a plate and sprinkle with lemon juice and sugar. Roll up and serve immediately.

Ice cream makes a really delightful addition.

Fab Fruity Flapjacks

Makes loads

These are irresistible and make a brilliant snack or quick breakfast because they are packed full of oats and fruit to keep you going until lunchtime.

Shopping List

250g butter
100g golden syrup
150g brown sugar
350g porridge oats
1 Granny Smith apple, grated
100g fresh blueberries

Preheat the oven to 190°C / fan oven 170°C / Gas Mark 5.

Grease a 20cm square cake tin with a small knob of the butter.

Melt the remaining butter gently in a large saucepan.

Remove from the heat.

Add all the other ingredients apart from the blueberries and mix well.

Put about half the mixture in the tin and press down well.

Tip the blueberries into the cake tin, spreading them out into an even layer, then spoon the remaining flapjack mixture on top, pressing down gently but firmly.

Bake for about 25 minutes, until golden brown.

Remove from the oven and leave to cool completely. It's a good idea to place in the fridge before removing from the tin as this makes it easier to cut into slices.

No-Bake Fridge Cake

Enough to feed a house of chocaholics

A truly blissful, indulgent treat that doesn't even need baking – and it will satisfy even the strongest chocolate craving!

Shopping List

150g butter, cut into pieces

150g plain chocolate, broken into pieces

2 tbsp golden syrup

225g digestive biscuits, crushed (but leave some good-sized chunks for texture)

25g chopped hazelnuts

25g raisins

Put the butter, chocolate and syrup into a saucepan and melt very slowly and gently over a low heat.

Stir in the crushed biscuits, nuts and raisins, mixing well.

Spread the mixture into a 20cm square cake tin and refrigerate for approximately 2-3 hours or even overnight.

Cut into pieces and spoil yourself.

'A little too much chocolate is just about right'

Fat Rascals

Makes one large round to be cut into pieces

You won't be able to resist these wonderful, fruity scones. As their name suggests they are slightly naughty, definitely addictive and smell absolutely delicious when they come out of the oven. A guaranteed hit when you yearn for a toothsome treat or when you want to spoil someone special.

Shopping List

A few drops of vegetable oil, for greasing

225g self-raising flour

½ teaspoon salt

50g margarine

50g caster sugar

1 large baking apple, peeled and chopped into small pieces

110g sultanas

1 egg, beaten

Preheat the oven to 200°C / fan oven 180°C / Gas Mark 7.

Grease a baking tray with the vegetable oil.

Sift the flour and salt into a mixing bowl.

Rub the margarine into the flour with your fingertips until it looks like breadcrumbs.

Stir in the sugar, apple and sultanas.

Add the beaten egg to form a soft dough, using your hands to bring it together.

Form the dough into a round shape and place onto the baking tray.

Gently mark into wedges with a knife (don't cut right through).

Bake for about 25 minutes until well risen and golden.

'Life is uncertain... eat dessert first'

Jumbles
Makes about 9

These buttery pale biscuits melt in the mouth and with the delicate taste of almonds and a hint of lemon they are the ultimate treat after a hard day studying.

Shopping List

75g butter

75g sugar

1 egg

150g self-raising flour

1 level tsp lemon zest

25g ground almonds

Preheat the oven to 180°C / fan oven 160°C / Gas Mark4.

In a mixing bowl, beat the butter and sugar together with a wooden spoon until pale and fluffy.

Add half the egg and mix well.

Sift in the flour, then add the lemon zest, almonds and remaining egg. Stir thoroughly until it begins to bind together.

Draw the dough together with your hands, then shape into a large flat sausage and cut into 9 pieces. Place these onto a greased baking sheet and form them into 'S' shapes or crescent shapes.

Bake in the oven for 12-15 minutes. Cool on a baking sheet for a few minutes then transfer to a wire cooling rack (or clean grill rack) to cool completely.

Bread & Butter Pudding

Serves 4-6 - leftovers are lovely cold

A heavenly pudding that can easily be made from what you have in the fridge and store cupboard.

Shopping List

75g butter, softened

Approximately 8 thin slices of bread with crusts

Handful of raisins or currants

2 eggs

450ml milk (substitute with some cream for a really luxurious pud)

75g soft brown sugar

Finely grated zest from ½ lemon (the yellow part of the skin which can be grated using a fine grater, but don't include the white pith as this is bitter)

½ tsp ground nutmeg

Preheat the oven to 180°C / fan oven 160°C / Gas Mark 4. Grease a large baking dish with a knob of the butter.

Butter the bread, cut into triangles and arrange half of them in the dish. Sprinkle the raisins or currants over the top, then cover with the remaining bread.

Whisk the eggs in a jug or bowl, then add the milk, sugar and lemon zest and mix well. Leave for a few minutes to give the sugar time to dissolve.

Pour this over the bread and sprinkle over some nutmeg and a little extra sugar and bake for 30-40 minutes until the pudding has risen and is just firm to the touch.

Serve warm, perhaps with a little cream…

Baked Bananas

A traditional Jamaican recipe that really needs nothing apart from a banana and whatever you wish to add. It is sweet and delicious and you will be coming back for more.

Preheat the oven to 180°C / fan oven 160°C / Gas Mark 4.

Place unpeeled banana on a foil-lined baking sheet.

Place in oven and cook for 15 minutes.

The skin will turn black, but don't panic.

Bring carefully out of the oven and allow to cool for a few minutes.

Transfer to a dish and split the skin lengthways with a sharp vegetable knife.

Add a generous scoop of ice cream (or a dollop of yoghurt or cream) on the side and using a spoon, eat the baked banana from its skin.

Shopping List (per person)

1 banana

Ice cream, Greek yoghurt or just cream, to accompany

Time flies like an arrow; fruit flies like a banana' – Groucho Marx

Coffee & Walnut Cake

This is sheer bliss in a cake and it is a good opportunity to use any spare walnut pieces there may be left over from the 'Wonderful Waldorf Salad'.

Shopping List

- 18cm cake tin (loose-based if possible)
- 125g softened butter (i.e. at room temperature)
- 125g caster sugar
- 2 large eggs
- 125g self-raising flour
- 1 tsp baking powder
- 2 tbsp coffee granules or powder, dissolved in 4 tbsp boiling water
- 80g walnuts, chopped

Preheat the oven to 170°C / fan oven 150°C / Gas Mark 3. Line the cake tin with greaseproof paper or grease it using the butter wrapper.

Beat the butter and sugar together (if you have a hand-held electric mixer this is easier, if not, use a wooden spoon and elbow grease!)

Gradually add the eggs, beating well between each addition.

Sift the flour and baking powder into the mixture, folding it in gently with a large metal spoon.

Add 1 tbsp of the coffee mixture, mixing well, then add about half of the remaining coffee mixture, stirring gently until the mixture has a soft dropping consistency.

Add the walnuts, stirring gently. Spoon into the cake tin and level the surface.

Bake for about 40 minutes. To check that it is cooked, insert a fine skewer into the centre – it should come out cleanly when the cake is cooked, so if it doesn't simply return to the oven and check again in 5-6 minutes. Cool completely.

For the icing

150g softened butter
(i.e. at room temperature)

Approximately 150g
icing sugar

For the icing, beat the butter until soft then gradually beat in the icing sugar. Add the remaining coffee mixture a little at a time (test until you are happy with the flavour).

When the cake has cooled, cut into 2 slices horizontally. Sandwich together with a generous half of the icing then spread the remaining icing on top.

Slice into generous wedges and serve to friends with a nice cuppa for a real afternoon-tea treat.

'Map out your future, but do it in pencil.' – Jon Bon Jovi

Carrot Cake

A divinely moist cake that has a natural sweetness provided by the carrots – it's so easy to make that there is a danger it may become a weekly student staple – but who cares?

Shopping List

2 medium eggs

80g soft brown sugar

5 tbsp vegetable oil

100g self-raising flour

150g carrots, finely grated

50g desiccated coconut

75g raisins

1 tsp ground cinnamon

1 tsp ground nutmeg

For the frosting

200g cream cheese

50g icing sugar

Preheat the oven to 190°C / fan oven 170°C / Gas Mark 5.

Line an 18cm square or round cake tin with greaseproof paper.

Whisk the eggs together (using a hand-held electric mixer if you have one) and then add the sugar. Continue whisking until thick and creamy – this will take about 5 minutes. Continue to whisk, slowly adding the oil.

Add the remaining ingredients and mix together thoroughly with a large spoon. The mixture will look rather lumpy and un-cake like, but that's okay.

Spoon into the cake tin and bake in the oven for about 35-40 minutes. Make sure it is firm to the touch before bringing it out of the oven. Allow to cool. The cake will be delicious as it is but if you wish, it can be finished off with cream cheese frosting.

To make the frosting, simply beat the cream cheese with the icing sugar until smooth. Place the cake on a plate and pile the frosting on top, spreading it out evenly to cover the surface.

Raspberry Muffins

Makes 12

Luscious, 'light as a feather' muffins which smell divine whilst cooking and will disappear very quickly once they come out of the oven.

Shopping List

75g butter

200g plain flour

70g caster sugar

2 teaspoons baking powder

½ teaspoon bicarbonate of soda

1 large egg, beaten

1 heaped tbsp natural yoghurt

200g raspberries

Finely grated zest from ½ lemon

A greased bun tray or bun cases in a bun tray

Preheat the oven to 200°C / fan oven 180°C / Gas Mark 6.

Melt the butter gently in a pan and put aside.

Mix all the dry ingredients in a large bowl.

In a separate bowl combine the egg, yoghurt and melted butter.

Pour the egg mixture into the dry ingredients and using a wooden spoon, combine gently and quickly. Don't be tempted to over mix, there **should** be lumps, don't worry!

Gently mix in the raspberries and lemon zest.

Spoon the mixture into 12 bun cases or into a non-stick bun tray and bake for 20 minutes. When done they will be golden and just firm to the touch.

'Just about a month from now I'm set adrift, with a diploma for a sail and lots of nerve for oars.' – Richard Halliburton

Index

'The best is yet to come'